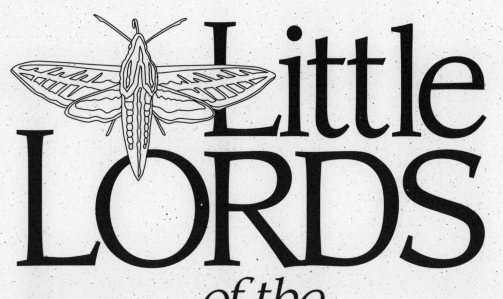

Little
LORDS
of the
Desert

Coloring/Learning
BOOK

Watch your step in the desert!

♡ Reading

Conrad Storad 2022

Written by Conrad J. Storad & Illustrated by Donna S. Atwood

ISBN 0-9660293-2-1

Published by Donna Atwood Design,
Phoenix, Arizona.

All illustrations by Donna S. Atwood.

Design, typesetting, and prepress production
by Donna Atwood Design.

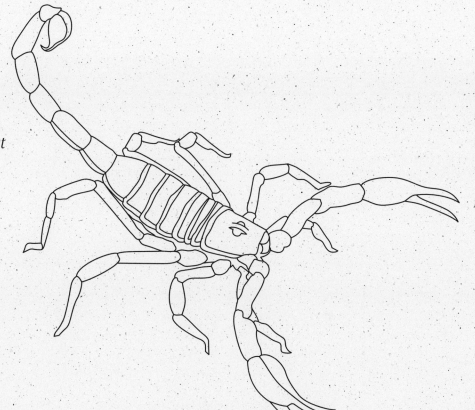

With deep respect for the natural beauty throughout our country and world, this book is printed on 100% recycled paper.

For Nichole, Breanna, and young readers of all ages. Always respect and appreciate the beautiful and unique creatures and plants that live in the deserts of our world. Never stop reading. Never stop learning!

– Conrad J. Storad

TABLE OF CONTENTS

Six Legs & Eight Legs

Insects. Arachnids. Just fancy names for bugs... correct? Nope. Not at all. Insects and arachnids are cousins. They both belong to the largest group of animals now living on the Earth. Arthropoda is the scientific name for this group, which scientists call a phylum. Animals in the group are called arthropods. Insects and arachnids are both types of arthropods. But they still are very different kinds of animals. The phylum Arthropoda includes centipedes, millipedes, arachnids such as spiders and scorpions, crustaceans such as crabs, shrimp, and lobsters, and insects.

People confuse insects and arachnids because they often look similar. For example, both insects and arachnids have segmented bodies and many walking legs. Unlike humans, both types of animals have no bones on the insides of their bodies. Instead of an inside skeleton, both insects and arachnids have tough outside body armor. This tough, hard shell is called an exoskeleton.

Insects and arachnids share some other similarities as well. But they really are not the same at all. There are important differences. Luckily, there are some easy ways to tell the difference between an insect and an arachnid. Use the following list to help learn the differences for yourself.

PHYLUM ARTHROPODA
- Class Insecta: Includes beetles, flies, bees, crickets, grasshoppers, moths, butterflies, wasps, mantids, cockroaches, etc.
- Class Arachnida: Includes spiders, scorpions, mites, and ticks.

WHAT IS AN INSECT?
- Insects have three major body sections: head, thorax, and abdomen.
- Head contains the eyes, mouthparts, and one pair of antennae.
- Six walking legs attach at the thorax.
- One or two pair of wings attach at the thorax.
- One set of large compound eyes.

WHAT IS AN ARACHNID?
- Arachnids have only two major body sections: cephalothorax and abdomen.
- Head and thorax are fused to form the cephalothorax.
  - Eight walking legs.
  - Thin waist connects two body parts.
  - Many eyes. As many as six or eight.
  - No antennae.
  - No wings.

Who Is in Charge of Planet Earth?

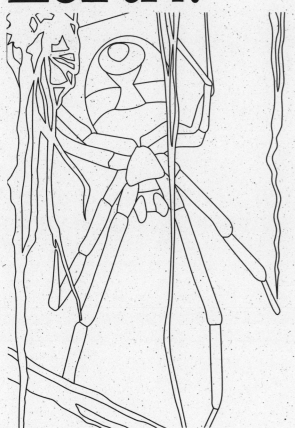

More than 6 billion people are alive today on our planet. But who truly rules the Earth? If numbers alone are used as the measuring tool, people do not come close to being in charge. Insects and arachnids are the masters of the forests and plains, the kings and queens of the jungles, the lords and ladies of the deserts, the true rulers of the world.

Insects and arachnids come in all shapes and sizes. The little creatures have people outnumbered by a huge margin. Scientists estimate that there are more than 1 quintillion individual insects and arachnids creeping and crawling and flying and buzzing around on any given day. A quintillion is a massive number. To be exact, you must write a numeral 1 followed by a string of 18 zeros. It looks like this: 1,000,000,000,000,000,000

That is a lot of bugs! But exactly how many creatures is 1 quintillion? Consider these facts. For each and every living human being, there are hundreds of millions of bugs and spiders. In 1968, scientists calculated that all of the insects and spiders alive on the Earth at that time would weigh more than 27 billion tons – more than 12 times the weight of the 3 billion human beings alive at that time.

Today, even if the total number of insects and arachnids has not increased in 30 years, the little creatures still outweigh humanity by a factor of six to one.

No matter how you think about it, there are lots of bugs on this planet. They live and eat and reproduce and fight and die as part of alien empires that exist all around us. Insects and arachnids have been around much longer than people. Their relatives were crawling around long before the first dinosaurs ever walked the Earth. Insects have been around for more than 300 million years. Arachnid ancestors swam in warm seas more than 600 million years ago.

To date, scientists have identified and described more than 1.2 million different kinds of animals on the Earth. More than 900,000 of those creatures are insects. More than 60,000 others are arachnids. Beyond a few sketchy details, we know very little about most of these amazing, beautiful, bizarre, creepy, colorful, and weird creatures. Even more amazing, scientists think that there may be as many as 30 million more kinds of insects and thousands of types of arachnids yet to be discovered.

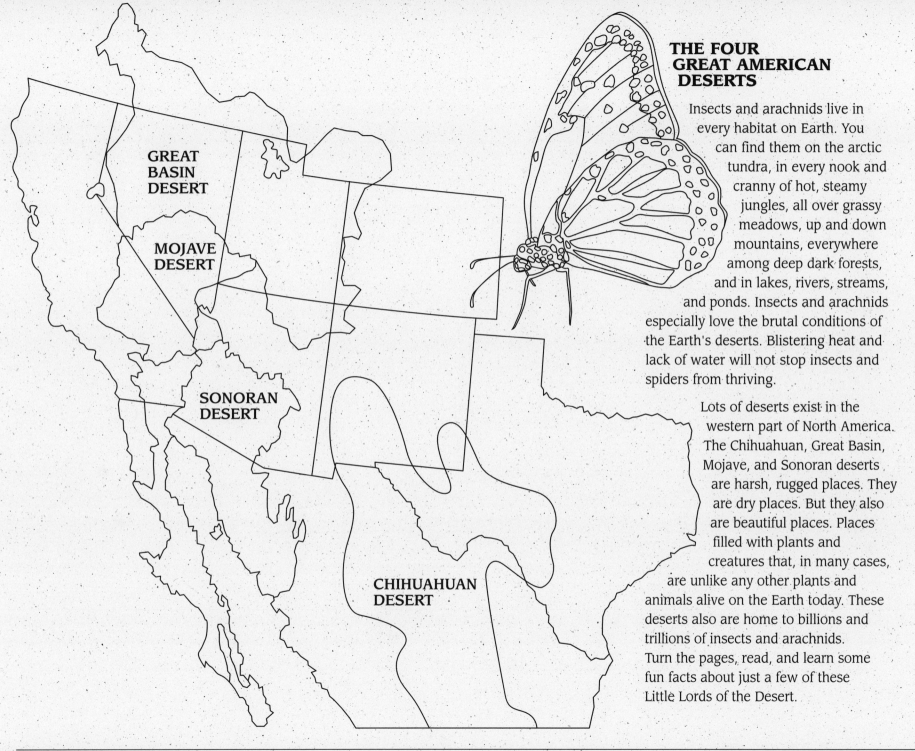

THE FOUR GREAT AMERICAN DESERTS

GREAT BASIN DESERT

MOJAVE DESERT

SONORAN DESERT

CHIHUAHUAN DESERT

Insects and arachnids live in every habitat on Earth. You can find them on the arctic tundra, in every nook and cranny of hot, steamy jungles, all over grassy meadows, up and down mountains, everywhere among deep dark forests, and in lakes, rivers, streams, and ponds. Insects and arachnids especially love the brutal conditions of the Earth's deserts. Blistering heat and lack of water will not stop insects and spiders from thriving.

Lots of deserts exist in the western part of North America. The Chihuahuan, Great Basin, Mojave, and Sonoran deserts are harsh, rugged places. They are dry places. But they also are beautiful places. Places filled with plants and creatures that, in many cases, are unlike any other plants and animals alive on the Earth today. These deserts also are home to billions and trillions of insects and arachnids. Turn the pages, read, and learn some fun facts about just a few of these Little Lords of the Desert.

ARIZONA BLISTER BEETLE
(Lytta magister)

Size: 5/8 inch to 1 1/8 inches long.
Color: Blue-black body with orange head and thorax. Legs are brownish red.
Habitat: Desert washes and hilltops.
Food: Desert shrubs. Brittlebush flowers and leaves are a favorite food.

The bright orange color of the Arizona Blister Beetle is a warning to birds and other predators. The warning is simple: "Eat me and you will get hurt." The Blister Beetle is armed with a powerful chemical called canthariden. The chemical burns the mouth of birds and other predators. It is strong enough to cause blisters on human skin. One experience with a nasty tasting Blister Beetle is enough to keep predators from coming back for seconds. Arizona Blister Beetles love to chew on the flowers and leaves of brittlebush and other desert shrubs. The beetle's larvae chow down on grasshopper eggs found in desert soil.

BEE ASSASSIN
(Apiomerus)

Size: 1/2 inch to 5/8 inch long.
Color: Red with blackish-brown markings on the shell.
Habitat: Meadows, grassy fields, and gardens.
Food: Insects of all kinds, especially bees.

Assassin bugs are found throughout North America. The Bee Assassin is most common in the West and gets its name from the manner in which it catches and kills other insects. The Bee Assassin lays in wait on the leaves or petals of colorful flowers waiting for honeybees and other pollinators to land. When the bee is busy gathering pollen, the Bee Assassin pounces.

It grabs the bee with its powerful forelegs. Then it drives its sharp beak-like mouth into the bee's back, injecting strong fluids. The fluids digest the insides of the unlucky bee. The Assassin then sucks out the digested goo.

BLACK WIDOW SPIDER
(Latrodectus hesperus)

Size: 1/2 inch to
         1 inch long, female.
         Male is much smaller.
Color: Shiny black body with
         bright red hourglass marking
         on the abdomen.
Habitat: Dark, secluded spots
         under rocks and logs and
         abandoned rodent burrows.
Food: Flies, moths, mosquitoes, ants,
         beetles, and other spiders.

The Black Widow is the most feared of all spiders. The female spider has venom that is very poisonous to people. The bite is extremely painful, but few people have actually died from a Black Widow bite. Other stories about the Black Widow are also untrue. The female does not always eat the male after mating. Only when the male is weak or near death does the female eat him. She would much rather eat insects trapped in her sticky, tangled webs. The spider injects powerful digestive fluids into the body of its prey which partially digest their insides. The Black Widow then feeds by sucking out the gooey bug juice.

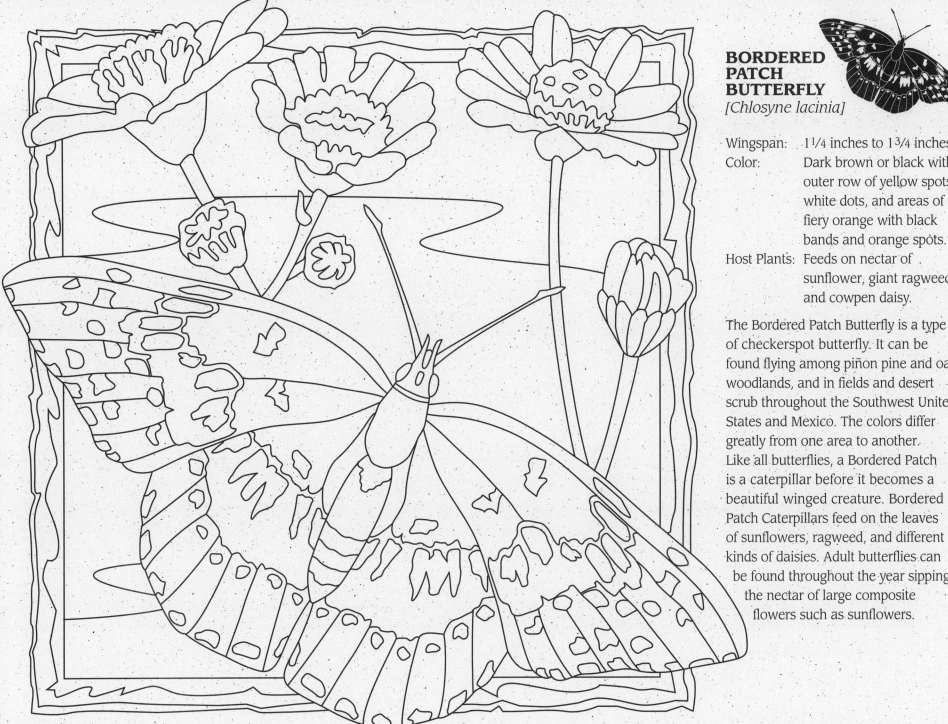

BORDERED PATCH BUTTERFLY
[Chlosyne lacinia]

Wingspan: 1 1/4 inches to 1 3/4 inches.
Color: Dark brown or black with outer row of yellow spots, white dots, and areas of fiery orange with black bands and orange spots.
Host Plants: Feeds on nectar of sunflower, giant ragweed, and cowpen daisy.

The Bordered Patch Butterfly is a type of checkerspot butterfly. It can be found flying among piñon pine and oak woodlands, and in fields and desert scrub throughout the Southwest United States and Mexico. The colors differ greatly from one area to another. Like all butterflies, a Bordered Patch is a caterpillar before it becomes a beautiful winged creature. Bordered Patch Caterpillars feed on the leaves of sunflowers, ragweed, and different kinds of daisies. Adult butterflies can be found throughout the year sipping the nectar of large composite flowers such as sunflowers.

CARPENTER BEE
(Xylocopa)

Size: 3/4 inch to 1 inch long.
Color: Dark black with reflections
         of green or blue.
Habitat: Forests, grassy fields
         and meadows.
Food: Nectar and pollen of
         many flowering plants.

The Carpenter Bee has a fat, black body. It looks much like a bumblebee. Most kinds of bees actually live alone. Only a few types of bees live in large groups, or hives. The Carpenter Bee is named for its ability to eat through wood with strong mouthparts. A Carpenter Bee can chew a tunnel as deep as a foot into the dry wood of houses or dead trees. In the deserts, Carpenter Bees build nests in the soft stalks of agave or yucca plants. The nest is a series of cells. The bee lines each cell with a paste made of pollen and nectar. Carpenter Bees protect their nests. They will chase birds and people if they get too close.

DRONE FLY
(Eristalis tenax)

Size: 5/8 inch long.
Color: Dark brown to
          black with yellow
          bands on abdomen.
          Wings are clear with
          brown blotches.
Habitat: Fields and meadows.
Food: Nectar and pollen from
          daisies, verbena,
          and poppies.

The Drone Fly is one member of a family of insects called syrphid flies. These flies resemble honeybees, bumblebees, or wasps of many kinds. They are called flower flies or hover flies, because they often hover over or rest on flowers where they feed on nectar and pollen. The Drone Fly looks like a fat honeybee. It has huge eyes that cover most of its head, a shiny thorax, and yellow stripes on its body. The Drone Fly does not sting or bite. But it will fly long distances to find flowers.

GIANT DESERT CENTIPEDE
(Scolopendra heros)

Size: 6 inches to 1 foot long.
Color: Blue-green or olive-green body segments, yellow legs, with black head and tail, and orange antennae.
Habitat: Dark places beneath rocks, rotting logs, and dead cactus.
Food: Insects, spiders, worms, snails, mice, toads, and small lizards.

The Giant Desert Centipede is not an easy creature to see, unless you like looking under rocks, rotting logs, or piles of leaves. Some centipedes have as many as 346 legs. The Giant Desert Centipede's body is made up of 21 segments. One pair of legs is attached to each segment. All centipedes are nocturnal, which means they are active at night. Giant Desert Centipedes can grow to be almost a foot long. The first pair of legs is modified to work much like jaws with fangs. Centipedes use their fangs to inject venom into the bodies of small insects, snails, worms, and spiders. Giant Desert Centipedes are big enough to attack and eat mice, toads, and small lizards.

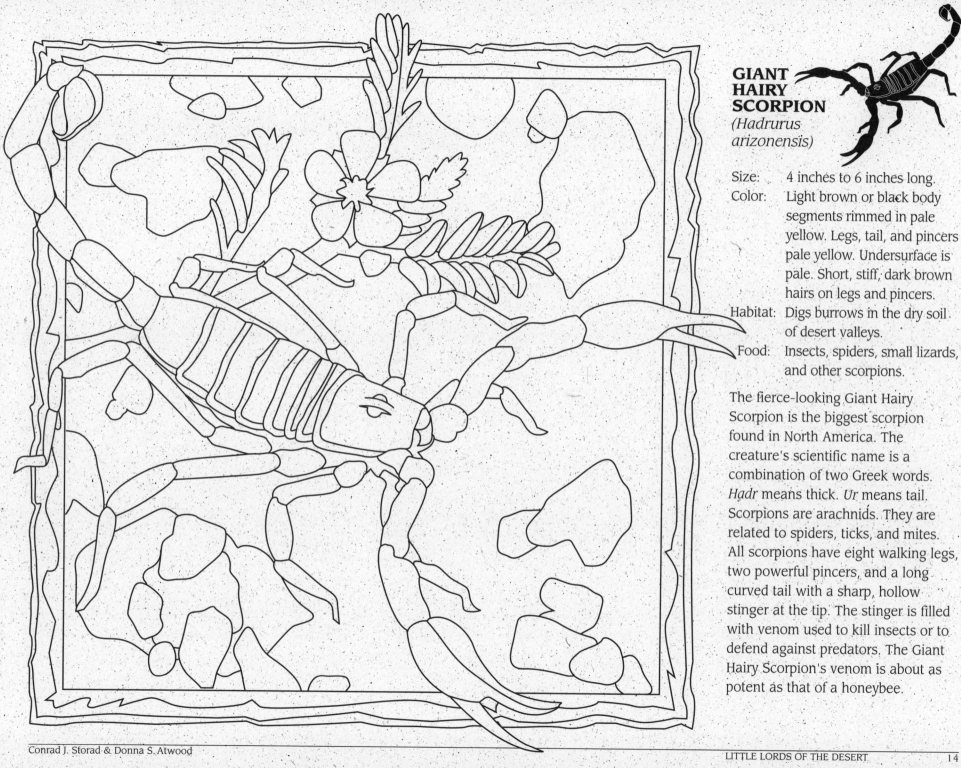

GIANT HAIRY SCORPION
(Hadrurus arizonensis)

Size: 4 inches to 6 inches long.

Color: Light brown or black body segments rimmed in pale yellow. Legs, tail, and pincers pale yellow. Undersurface is pale. Short, stiff, dark brown hairs on legs and pincers.

Habitat: Digs burrows in the dry soil of desert valleys.

Food: Insects, spiders, small lizards, and other scorpions.

The fierce-looking Giant Hairy Scorpion is the biggest scorpion found in North America. The creature's scientific name is a combination of two Greek words. *Hadr* means thick. *Ur* means tail. Scorpions are arachnids. They are related to spiders, ticks, and mites. All scorpions have eight walking legs, two powerful pincers, and a long curved tail with a sharp, hollow stinger at the tip. The stinger is filled with venom used to kill insects or to defend against predators. The Giant Hairy Scorpion's venom is about as potent as that of a honeybee.

GIANT VINEGARONE
(Matigoproctus giganteus)

Size: 3 inches long, body only.
          6 inches, from head
          to tip of tail.
Color: Many shades of brown
          or dark black.
Habitat: Digs burrows under logs
          and rotting wood, piles
          of branches or debris.
Food: Insects and small spiders.

The Giant Vinegarone is sometimes called a whip scorpion. It holds a long, thin tail curled forward over its back. The creature is a cousin to spiders and scorpions. It has four pairs of walking legs and two strong pedipalps that act as pincers. It also has eight eyes, two in front and three along each side of its head. The Vinegarone cannot sting, but it can pinch. It hunts only at night. When disturbed by an enemy, the Vinegarone sprays a mist from a gland at the base of its tail. The mist smells like vinegar. It contains an acid that attacks the waxy coating on the exoskeletons of spiders and insects.

GRAND WESTERN CICADA
(Tibicen dorsata)

Size: 1 3/8 inches to 2 inches long. Wings spread to 4 3/8 inches.

Color: Brown-black or greenish. body with yellow on thorax. Wings are brownish-green.

Habitat: Grasslands, woods and forests.

Food: Adults do not eat. Young suck juice from roots of plants.

On summer nights in the desert, the humming, buzzing chorus is usually provided by cicadas. The cicada "sings" by vibrating thin, drum-like membranes on its abdomen. Cicadas are large insects with big heads, stout bodies, and two pairs of wings. The Grand Western Cicada is the biggest and most colorful cicada found in the desert. Some cicadas appear every year at midsummer. Adult cicadas live for only a few weeks. Other kinds appear only after their young have lived many years underground. The most famous is the 17-Year Cicada, which lives only in the United States. The Grand Western Cicada appears every summer in the same area.

GREEN DARNER DRAGONFLY
(Anex junius)

Wingspan: 2 3/4 inches to 4 3/8 inches.
Color: Thorax is bright green. Abdomen is blue to purplish-gray. Large chocolate-brown eyes. Wings are pale with yellowish tips.
Habitat: Wet areas near creeks, streams, ponds, and rivers.
Food: Mosquitoes, gnats, midges, and other flying insects.

The Green Darner Dragonfly is the largest of many kinds of dragonflies that live in and around deserts. All dragonflies live near streams, creeks, rivers, and wet oasis areas. The Green Darner is one of the best and fastest flyers of the insect world. All dragonflies have four powerful wings that each move independently. As a result, dragonflies can hover like helicopters. They also can fly and turn in an instant both forward and backward. The Green Darner is sometimes called the Snake Doctor or Darning Needle. It zooms low above the water to snatch midges, flies, and mosquitoes right from the air.

HORSE LUBBER GRASSHOPPER
(Taeniopoda eques)

Size: 1 ½ inches to 2 ½ inches long.

Color: Shiny black with large splotches of orange or yellow.

Habitat: Desert grasslands and wooded areas.

Food: Leaves of mesquite trees, desert shrubs, and flowers.

The Horse Lubber Grasshopper has a thick, stout black body with colorful orange or yellow markings. The grasshopper's fore wings have bright yellow veins. The hind wings have red-and-black borders. The male Horse Lubber can fly for very short distances. Adults are seen most often in late summer until November. They munch on the leaves of mesquite trees and other desert trees and shrubs. Male Horse Lubbers make a buzzing sound by rapidly snapping their fore wings together. When disturbed, they jump into bushes or clumps of grass to hide.

IRONCLAD BEETLE

(Zopherus haldemani)

Size: 3/4 inch to 1 inch long.

Color: Head, body, and wing covers are dull ivory-yellow with black spots.

Habitat: Desert floor and rocky crevices.

Food: Scavenge on rotting wood and dead plants.

The Ironclad Beetle has an extremely hard body. It looks like a tiny spotted tank with yellow marks on its black legs. Not much is known about the life cycle of Ironclad Beetles. They are nocturnal. When the sun goes down, Ironclad Beetles come out of dark crevices between rocks to chew on rotting wood or dead plants. These beetles are masters at conserving water. When disturbed by a nosy pack rat or grasshopper mouse, the Ironclad Beetle will play dead. The insect's hard shell makes it a difficult meal. Most predators will search for something softer to eat.

JERUSALEM CRICKET
(Stenopelmatus fuscus)

Size: 1 1/8 inches to 2 inches long.
Color: Shiny amber-brown with dark brown bands on abdomen.
Habitat: Lives under rocks on desert hillsides, on sand dunes, and is often found in the nests of desert pack rats.
Food: Other insects, decaying plant matter, and plant roots.

The Jerusalem Cricket is scary looking because it has a thick humpbacked body and a large head with powerful jaws. It is harmless to humans.

Jerusalem Crickets also have very long antennae and short stubby legs. They do not have wings. Jerusalem Crickets are active during both day and night. But they are very slow-moving creatures. They make a "scratchy" noise by rubbing together their hind legs. In Arizona and New Mexico, members of the Navajo Indian Tribe have a special name for the Jerusalem Cricket. They call it Who-seh-tsinni, which means "Old Man Bald Head."

LARGE MILKWEED BUG
(Oncopeltus fasciatus)

Size: 3/8 inch to 5/8 inch long.
Color: Black body with bright red or orange markings on the thorax. Wings are black with bands of orange or red.
Habitat: Grassy fields or meadows.
Food: Seeds of milkweed plants.

The bodies of Large Milkweed Bugs look like long, colorful ovals. The insect sometimes sips nectar from flowers in fields and gardens. But its favorite food is the growing seeds of the milkweed plant. The Large Milkweed Bug inserts the sharp point of its tube-like mouth into the soft flesh of developing milkweed seeds. It greedily sucks out all the sap it can hold. Milkweed Bugs are excellent flyers. When the food supply gets low, the insects fly off in large clouds to find new fields of milkweed plants. Milkweed Bugs can fly long distances to find food.

MEXICAN QUEEN BUTTERFLY

(Danaus gilippus strigosus)

Wingspan: 3 inches to 3 3/4 inches.
Color: Bright reddish-brown wings. Wide black trim and fine black veins and white spots on the long fore wings. Underside is similar but darker brown with heavier black veins.
Host Plant: Milkweed.

The Queen Butterfly looks much like a chocolate-brownish version of the famous monarch butterfly. The adult Queen Butterfly feeds on the nectar of milkweed plants. Most birds avoid eating the Queen Butterfly and the monarch because poisons in the milkweed nectar make them taste awful. Viceroy butterflies often mimic both the Queen and the monarch butterflies to gain protection from birds. The large caterpillar of a Queen Butterfly has stripes of dark brown and white with yellow spots. It feeds on the poisonous leaves of milkweed plants.

MEXICAN RED KNEE TARANTULA
(Brachypelma smithi)

Size: 2 ½ to 4 inches long,
         leg tip to leg tip.
Color: Velvet black with bright
         patches of reddish-orange
         on legs.
Habitat: Dry desert soil and
         rocky scrubland.
Food: Insects, small lizards,
         mice, grub worms, and
         other spiders.

The colorful Mexican Red Knee is the favorite spider for people who keep tarantulas as pets. There are more than 800 different kinds of tarantulas in the world. Most are very shy creatures. Tarantulas defend themselves in different ways. But most would rather hide in a snug burrow dug into desert soil or inside a tube web built high in a jungle tree. All tarantulas have large, sharp fangs filled with strong venom. The Red Knee also uses its body hairs like tiny poison darts. When threatened by a predator, the spider rubs its body vigorously with a back leg. Clouds of tiny hairs fly into the air. The stinging hairs irritate the eyes and noses of enemies, giving the spider time to run away.

OBSCURE GROUND MANTID
(Litaneutria obscura)

Size: 5/8 inch to 1 1/8 inches long.
Color: Gray body. Wings are sooty gray with a brown spot.
Habitat: Dry desert grasslands.
Food: Ants, beetles, aphids, and other small insects.

The Obscure Ground Mantid is much smaller than its larger and more famous cousin, the praying mantis. All mantids are superb hunters. They have long slender bodies, triangular heads with huge eyes and long antennae, and muscular forelegs lined with sharp spines. The forelegs are perfectly designed for grabbing and holding on to prey. Mantids hunt by ambush. The Obscure Ground Mantid finds a spot in the grass or on a twig then waits patiently for an ant or beetle to walk within reach. Quicker than you can blink an eye, the mantid grabs the prey and holds it in a vice-like grip. Then it chews the bug to bits with powerful jaws.

ORNATE TIGER MOTH
(Apantesis ornata)

Wingspan: 1 1/4 inches to 1 5/8 inches.

Color: Black fore wings are crosshatched with ivory-white. Hind wings are pink or red with dark black spots. Black furry body with streaks of white on thorax. Abdomen is brownish-yellow.

Host Plants: Adults sip nectar of night-blooming desert flowers.

Tiger moths have furry bodies with brightly colored wings. The bright colors serve as a warning to birds and other predators. "Don't eat me, because I taste very nasty." The Ornate Tiger Moth likes to fly at night. Male moths are attracted to artificial lights. Female moths like to stay near night-blooming desert flowers such as yucca and cereus. The caterpillar for this moth is mostly black. It has pale spots on both sides of a thin yellow stripe that runs down the middle of its body.

PALO VERDE BEETLE
(Prionus heroicus)

Size: 1 inch to 2 inches long.
Color: Dark brown to black with a metallic sheen.
Habitat: Desert soil near roots of Palo Verde trees.
Food: Adults eat decaying plant matter. Larvae feed on the roots of desert trees.

The Palo Verde Beetle is also called the Palo Verde Root Borer, or Prionus Beetle. The insect has very long, thick antennae. The adult beetle is dark metallic brown or black and can grow to almost two inches in length. Because of its size, the beetle is scary looking for people new to living in desert areas. People often mistake Palo Verde Beetles for giant sewer roaches. The Palo Verde Beetle's larva spends most of its life burrowed into the ground near the roots of Palo Verde trees. At night, adult beetles often are attracted to porch lights. They make loud thudding sounds when they fly into windows and screen doors.

POLYBIINE PAPER WASP
(Mischocyttarus flavitarsus)

Size: 5/8 inch long.
Color: Black body marked
        with bright yellow.
        Wings are pale amber.
Habitat: Found near fields of flowers,
        meadows, and sandy areas.
Food: Adults sip on nectar.
        Larvae eat caterpillars.

There are many kinds of paper wasps. Some live alone. Others form large nests with one queen and many workers, much like bees. All paper wasps can deliver a painful sting. The Polybiine Paper Wasp has a long waist called a pedicel. The pedicel connects the insect's bright black-and-yellow thorax and abdomen. Polybiine Paper Wasps usually work alone to build a nest. Sometimes females work together. But one wasp always takes charge. She eats the eggs of the other wasps. When her eggs hatch, she brings them caterpillars to eat. The mother wasp chews up the caterpillar before feeding it to her young.

TARANTULA HAWK WASP
(Hemipepsis)

Size: Body is 1/2 inch to 1 1/2 inches long.

Color: Shiny blue-black body with reddish-orange wings.

Habitat: Dry desert hillsides and valleys.

Food: Adults sip nectar of brittlebush. Larvae eat live spiders caught and paralyzed by the sting of adult wasp.

In the Southwestern deserts, Tarantula Hawk Wasps often grow larger than one inch long. They have very long stingers. Adult Tarantula Hawks actually sip the nectar of brittlebush and other desert flowers. They hunt spiders to provide food for their young. The Wasp will attack a tarantula or other large spider. The Wasp paralyzes the spider with the venom from its long stinger. It then digs a burrow and drags the spider's body inside. The Wasp lays a single egg on the body of the living spider, then seals the burrow. When the egg hatches a few days later, the Wasp larva has a fresh spider to eat.

TEXAS CARPENTER ANT
(Camponotus festinatus)

Size: ¾ inch to 1 inch long,
          worker ant.
Color: Brownish-yellow, sometimes
          with dark bands on abdomen.
          Dark brown-black antennae.
Habitat: Live in the dead wood of
          standing or fallen trees,
          utility poles, or under
          stones and cow dung.
Food: Other insects, honeydew,
          and juice from rotting fruit.

Carpenter Ants of many kinds live in
different habitats all over the world.
The Texas Carpenter Ant is found in
all the great deserts of North America.
It lives in large colonies that include
thousands of soldier ants and worker
ants of many different sizes. A queen
Carpenter Ant builds her nest in the
dry wood of dead or dying trees.
When the sun goes down, hundreds
of soldier Carpenter Ants march out
of the nest in search of food to feed
the queen and other members of the
colony. Sometimes they invade homes
looking for the sweet juice of rotting
fruit or vegetables. As they march,
Texas Carpenter Ants will attack and
kill other ants and insects of all kinds.

TIGER BEETLE
(Cicindela pulchra)

Size: ³/₈ inch to ³/₄ inch long.
Color: Body, antennae, and legs brilliant blue-green and orange with purple sheen.
Habitat: Desert floor among loose soil and rocks.
Food: Small beetles, ants, and termites.

Tiger Beetles come in many sizes and colors. They look like brightly colored jewels flashing across the desert floor. *Cicindela pulchra* does not have a common name. But it is one of the most brightly colored of all Tiger Beetles found in Arizona. It hunts for only a few hours each day. When the temperature gets too hot, it looks for a shady spot to cool down. All Tiger Beetles are hunters. They have excellent eyesight, long legs, and are very fast runners. Tiger Beetles use their large, sickle-shaped jaws to catch and crush smaller beetles, ants, small spiders, and other insects.

WESTERN TIGER SWALLOWTAIL
(Papilio rutulus)

Wingspan: 2 3/4 inches to 4 inches.
Color: Bright yellow wings with vertical black stripes. Wings have black trim with yellow and pale blue spots. Abdomen is black with yellow side stripes.
Host Plants: Milkweed, thistle, zinnia, lilac, and desert willow.

Second only to the bright orange monarch, the Tiger Swallowtail is one of the most recognized butterflies in North America. The Western Tiger Swallowtail usually is found flying near desert streams, creeks, and other wet areas during the spring and early summer. Adult butterflies like to sip the tasty nectar from desert flowers such as thistle, milkweed, lilac, zinnia, yerba santa, abelia, and desert willow. Tiger caterpillars love to chew the leaves of cottonwood, willow, and aspen trees.

WHITE-LINED SPHINX MOTH
(Hylus lineata)

Wingspan: 2 1/2 inches to 3 1/2 inches.

Color: Brown fore wings with white-lined veins. Hind wings have red-pink bands. Thorax is brown with six white stripes. Abdomen has series of alternating black-and-white spots on each side.

Host Plants: Datura, verbena, evening primrose, night-blooming cereus.

Sphinx Moths are often called Hawk Moths. They are very swift flyers and are found in many sizes and colors. The White-lined Sphinx Moth also has the ability to hover, much like a hummingbird. As it hovers in front of a blooming flower, the Sphinx Moth will uncoil its proboscis. The proboscis is a long, thin mouthpart that the moth uses much like a long straw or tubular tongue. White-lined Sphinx Moths fly at dusk or at night. They love to sip nectar from the night-blooming desert flowers such as datura, yucca, verbena, and evening primrose.